From Empty to Overflow:

5 Radical Actions Women Leaders Use to Rejuvenate, Grow Profits, and Inspire People

Jenny DuFresne

From Empty to Overflow

Jenny DuFresne

Dedication

To the women whose legacy I stand upon:
My mommy, Anni Beach
Grandma DuFresne
Great Grandma Stone
Great Great Grandma Jones
Great Grandma DuFresne
Great Aunt Burns
Great Grandma Johnson
Grandma Johnson

To all the women in my maternal and paternal lineage whose names and stories I do not know.

Thank you.

From Empty to Overflow

Jenny DuFresne

Table of Contents

Jenny DuFresne

From Empty to Overflow

Introduction

You are an amazing leader. You have built an amazing resume of impact and accomplishments. But let's be honest, your life's chaotic and frustrating. The stress and overwork have taken an emotional, physical, and spiritual toll. You <u>know</u> you need to make a change, but you're resistant. After all, you're a leader. You're doing what every leader you know is doing. But to lead powerfully, you need to lead from your energy overflow. The things you're doing right now rob you of your energy and deplete you. It's time to be intentional about your self-care so you can lead from your overflow. What is driving you? What is the cost? Are you invested in yourself as much as you are in your job or company? I know how this trap works because I've been *there. You tell yourself, "I have to do it". The truth is if you don't take care of yourself, you won't be able to do it. When you lead on empty—everything is impacted—purpose, profits, and people. Every human being you touch needs your brilliant gifts. It's time to take a radical stand for yourself. Right now!*

Chapter 1:

My Life Today

A few years ago, I could never imagine the life I live today. I never thought it possible. Today, I am living a life with more freedom, joy, happiness, and connection with people around me. Especially, the people I love and hold dear. Today, I enjoy wonderful physical vitality. My body is healthy and strong. Today, I find joy in the little things around me. Today, I'm more creative, inspired, and inquisitive about the things I produce and the actions I take.

I feel lighter—freer—like the world's weight lifted from my shoulders.

Freedom
Today my life is about freedom. It's about biting into life; enjoying the

juiciness life offers. I'm excited when I wake up in the morning. I wake up with intentionality. I first feed myself and then I feed the people I care about and love: my family and friends. Then the people I am privileged to touch and inspire in the world.

Today, my life is full in ways that I could never imagine. I'm a better friend. I'm a better daughter. As an entrepreneur, I enjoy building my company. I am privileged to coach leaders and entrepreneurs. A full 360 degrees, I'm a better human being. I listen more deeply, and I am more expressive. Today, my life is all about being fully present to life.

When I wake up in the morning, I spend time in my spiritual practice getting grounded in my body, spirit, and intuition—the things that keep me balanced throughout the day. I wake up to enjoy the beauty of nature.

At this moment, while writing, I'm watching the rain fall. It's so beautiful. This is the kind of intentionality that I create every single day. I watch the sun spreads its glory over the landscape and marvel at the beauty of that experience. I invest in my personal growth and development; growing who I am in the world and how I choose to touch the world. My relationships are stronger than they've been in years. I'm fully present and intentional.

Shift

As you read my story, you'll understand why all these things are is so important to me. You'll see why taking care of myself first, is so important—to me and to everyone around me. And why I created the experience to have wonderful adventures.

I made a radical change and shift in my life; in how I live and how I lead. Today, I lead from my overflow. But it wasn't always my truth. For years, I led completely depleted, drained, and exhausted.

Recently, I drove an hour to listen to people making music in the park. It was bright, sunny and beautiful. I didn't check my phone. I didn't do anything but breathe and be fully present in that moment. I often go hiking to admire Nature's smallest details.

These kinds of adventures are what make our lives extraordinary. They give us the space to refuel, rejuvenate, and replenish. But almost every woman leader I know is depleted, stressed-out, and frustrated. This way of being directly impacts three things: our purpose, profits, and people.

To be intentional about reconnecting to yourself, is the most powerful action you take as a leader. It supports you to be connected to your purpose. To be connected in a way that grows your profits in your business, and allows you to connect deeply and authentically to people around you.

Wouldn't you love a deeper connection to your family and your teams; to the people that make things happen around you; the people that bring you joy and inspiration? That is how my life is today. Every day I create ways I can make even deeper connections in my life.

In this book, I will share five actions that I discovered that are available to every leader. What I know is that work is often the all-consuming endeavor for women leaders. Work is voracious, like a piranha school, it consumes the Soul of life.

Work was never meant to consume our lives. When our every waking moment is consumed by work—our mind and body are dramatically depleted. We pay a terrible cost. This obsession—mania—blocks the sharing of our gifts. Our fixation with professional success does a tremendous disservice to the world.

A time will come when work ends. That's the experience I had. There's a time when going to a job ends—budget cuts, termination, restructuring, sickness. When it ends, and you're standing there, you look around, and everything is empty.

This is a profound, earth-shaking experience. A great resume NEVER brings joy, physical vitality, wonderful relationships, or love. A resume never laughs at a great memory or wraps its arms around you. A resume never tells you how much you're loved or appreciated.

Creating a life overflowing with energy, a life that is joy-filled, is an intentional act. No matter what you're doing, I'm convinced, really, I'm living proof, that you can create a life filled with extraordinary and joy-filled moments. How? You focus on the *living* part of life, not the career part of life. You're focused on the things that are most important to you. And by extension, you are better in all aspects of your life-including your profession.

Right now, you may be arguing with me. Telling me how important it is for you as a woman to have a professional career. I absolutely agree. What I'm sharing is not about NOT having a career or achieving great professional accolades. No, this book is a wake-up call. A vigorous shaking. A reminder to be deeply connected to your essence—to fill yourself so you lead from an overflow of vibrant energy.

Invitation
I'm glad you've joined me in this journey—an adventure, really. I invite

you to approach this conversation with an open heart and an open mind. No matter where you are as a leader—whether you are the leader in your family, Fortune 500 company, the mosque, synagogue, Ile, church, or the business builder, this book—my story—is designed for you.

We always role model for those around us. When we lead empty and depleted, when we lead frustrated, stressed, angry, or depressed, we directly impact people and profits. When we role model leading depleted, it becomes limiting and disconnecting for the people around us. As leaders, we know we influence people. Why not start lead from a place of energy overflow?

Why?
Our leadership roles are killing us. I don't think any woman wants to die because of her leadership role. No one wants to die alone. The meaning of our

lives is far beyond a great resume and shareholder value. But we've forgotten this truth. I share my story because it's time. Time to invent a new set of leadership competencies and centers on self-care as a primary competency.

This conversation takes courage. Why? Because I am defying a way of being that most leaders live and are entangled. I am defying the belief that getting ahead or being successful must look a certain way.

It is time to act and believe that to **live boldly in our purpose, to grow profits, and inspire people can ONLY happen when we lead from our overflow.** It is the only way. I don't want another leader to die physical, spiritual, or relational death because she never invested time in herself and her wellbeing.

That is what happened to me.

From Empty to Overflow

I believe women leaders have a profound calling to build, inspire, and create. I believe that now, more than ever, women leaders have an obligation to share our unique gifts with the world. I believe that we can only lead by **first** doing the things that replenish our energy.

It is in our deepest, darkest pain that we make profound discoveries. In my deep, desperate pain, I discovered five radical actions that guided me to lead differently. In this book, I share the five actions designed to guide you to create joy, happiness, and energy in your life. I believe this way of being will profoundly inspire your purpose, profits, and people.

Chapter 2:

The Big Wakeup Call

Over 10 years ago, I envisioned and built, what became a multimillion dollar organization. As I built the organization, barriers and obstacles seemed to be my best friends.

Two to three years in, I wasn't sleeping. I existed on coffee, a bite of food here and there, and adrenalin—massive amounts of adrenalin. My everyday stressors of building and leading the organization were so intense that my body began to rebel against how I was treating it. One day, my body gave me a smack down—crushed me.

Crushed
The day started around 4:00am.

From Empty to Overflow

Heart-pounding anxiety and stress with its iron grip on my neck and shoulders. Just another normal start to my day. My mind swirled. Every single detail of the day churned in my mind. Really, my mind was in overdrive—problem solving; creating a backup plan to the backup plan to the backup plan. A long day ahead.

I jumped in my car and raced to work. My mind swirling with all I had to do. A critical conversation with a leader in my organization had to happen. Today. I couldn't ignore it any longer. Ahead of me lay a finance meeting and budget review. Challenging financial decisions. Performance evaluations. Staff meetings. With a big swig of coffee, I bolted into the day.

As the day wrapped up, I called the leader into my office. Small talk. We had a significant issue with an employee. It was her responsibility to resolve. The problem had quickly eroded morale. But the leader seemed comfortable ignoring it all. "What are your plans to work with Mrs. Jones?" (not her real name), I asked anxiously. The leader leaned back in her chair; sized me up and flippantly said, "I don't know. I'm not going to do anything. What do you want me to do?"

In a flash, my blood pressure shot through the roof. I couldn't breathe. She's responsible for this mess! The thought swirled. Did she just glibly tell me she wasn't going to solve the problem? My mind—already stretched to its limits—searched for a solution. My head throbbed. My shoulders tightened like the skin on a drum. Iron tight.

I looked at my watch. I was going to be late for the fundraiser an hour across town. "We'll talk tomorrow." I barely made eye contact with her less she feel the full weight of my fury. I stuffed my laptop in my bag and ran to my car.

Traffic was horrible. I kept thinking, "The leader has no intention of solving the problem." My heart pounded. "Why is she here?" This was one of her many performance issues. "What is the solution?" I agonized over this question as I raced across town.

The fundraiser had started 15-minutes before I arrived. I despise being late. Especially today. This amazing opportunity. This gathering of our city's influential leaders—movers and shakers. The beautiful home made for an intimate setting. There I was, a leader of influence and impact, with other powerful leaders. I thought about the questions I had for the senator. This fundraiser was our opportunity to access this key decision-maker. There was a lot of work we needed to do that would need her influence.

I stood, chatting with my colleagues. A cold glass of orange juice in my right

Jenny DuFresne

hand. I swirled the juice hearing the ice cubes clank against the glass. I felt my body rock a bit, like I had a bit too much wine to drink. But I wasn't drinking alcohol. I hadn't eaten since early morning. I steadied myself—reaching to touch the wall to my left.   I leaned forward—closer—to   hear   what   my colleague was saying. Her voice seemed to moving away from me. It was difficult to hear. Except for a sudden, loud, thundering roar of a waterfall.

The roaring flooded my ears. From my peripheral vision, I noticed these huge gray curtains—on my left and right-- quickly pulled over my eyes. *Whooosh!*

There was a thud far, far away.

I felt fully refreshed when I woke up from my nap. As I opened my eyes, I was puzzled. Why were all these people in my bedroom?   As I became more alert, I realized I was **not** in my bedroom. No, I was in a crumpled heap on the floor of the senator's fundraiser. Me—the influential leader—on the floor of this powerful senator's fundraiser. A crumpled heap still holding the cup of orange juice in my hand.

I was shocked. Here I was, a trailblazing leader in a crumpled heap on the floor. My colleagues hovered over me. "Jenny, are you ok? Are you ok?" Their faces contorted with worry. "Call 911!", someone yelled.

The paramedics came. Rolling a gurney right into the middle of the senator's fundraiser. I saw her briefly glance my way. The look on her face. Not happy.

As the paramedics lifted the gurney into the ambulance, I kept asking to myself, "What is going on? What just happened?" I just couldn't put the pieces together. When I finally got to the hospital, I was all by myself. The doctors were furiously working on me. My heart rate was in the danger zone: beating incredibly fast. The doctors couldn't get it under control. They couldn't figure out why they were unable to bring my heart rate down.

Saline bag after saline bag, the doctors pumped the life-stabilizing liquid into my body. They put me through a zillion tests. Machines, tubes, beeps. Long, thin receipt-like paper show squiggly lines. My life lines. Several of my colleagues rushed into the emergency room an hour later. I smiled reassurance to them. "I'm okay," I insisted. But, really, I felt like I was outside of my body, looking down at the bizarre scene. I'm a warrior. I've always been invincible. Always.

"What just happened?" The question swirled in my head. The doctors weren't sure what was going on. Finally, my heart rate came down. No longer life-threatening. But the tests showed irregularities. Hours later, I was released. I realized my worst nightmare just happened.

Collusion

I had been "hit by a bus". I always told my board, "Listen, you guys need to know what to do. Because if I get hit by a bus, you have to carry the mission forward." I made leading depleted, empty, an acceptable and expected way of being. I was just "hit by a "bus". This was my wakeup call. I pushed myself beyond all limits—far beyond limits that anybody should ever ask of their body.

Does this story sound like anyone you know? Like many women leaders, we don't have just one wakeup call. We often have multiple wakeup calls before we **wake up** and realize that leading powerfully **cannot** mean that we lead bone dry, empty, depleted. Leading powerfully cannot mean that we burn ourselves out, that we sacrifice the most important thing in our lives. Life itself.

I was the leader that bought into a belief that I don't show breakdown or any sign of weakness. After my first ambulance ride ever, I didn't go to work for a week. Because I learned not to show weakness or vulnerability, only two people in my company knew what had happened. I came face-to-face with the tremendous health impact that my "see the hill, take the hill" actions had on my body.

Do you find yourself struggling and feeling like you really cannot rest and relax? Or maybe you find yourself saying, "I can't trust that my people will do this as well as I can." Are you stuck with the sense that you always must be perfect? This was me. Some self-conversations were conscious. Other questions percolated in the deep mines of my mind.

From Empty to Overflow

And what about my people? One of my deepest leadership values is to **lead by** example. Imagine what kind of example I was. My whole company was entangled in my belief system about work and sacrifice. My motto was, "see the hill, take the hill". I pushed myself relentlessly to build the company. I demanded the same from my team. Do you recognize this in leaders around you? Or yourself?

I wish I could tell you that I immediately changed my life after my health scare. But if you lead like I did, you know that isn't true. Absolutely, at that moment and several months after, I vowed to do better; to change my life and how I worked. But it took several more incidences—increasingly more life threatening—for a radical change to take place.

What if you create in your leadership role, an experience where you are refreshed, invigorated, and experience life/work harmony? What if you lead every day from your energy overflow? What if you create in your company or division, an opportunity for people to come to work excited, rejuvenated? Can you imagine what that would be like? The truth is, not only is it positive, but it is essential if you want your business to thrive. It's a key lever that you can create for your life.

No!

I've taken a stand, because I know the cost. The cost is life itself. No leader should lose her life to her job, her profession. No leader should lead empty. No leader should kill off her team.

Leading empty and depleted wasn't just a health cost. There was a huge cost to my team. It was a cost to our ability to grow. Even though we doubled in size every two years, there was a cost. There was a cost to my personal relationships, my friendships. Everything. I sacrificed everything. And at the end of the day, what I realized was that my belief about success was a faulty one. From empty to overflow requires a new definition of success.

Success

Success must *first* begin with radical self-care. A new definition of success must *first* embrace being happy, whole, and connected to what truly matters— our health, our spirit, our families, our friends, our important relationships. This is what I'm committed to manifesting in the world. Through partnerships with women leaders, my vision is to guide a redefinition of success.

As I've reflected on how I became a leader who drove herself to the edge of death, I began to see five glorifications that keep us from being our absolute best selves as leaders. Our leadership culture worships the five glorifications.

And dramatically penalizes any leader who dares to defy this broken norm. But, we must craft and lead a new way.

From Empty to Overflow

Chapter 3:

The 5 Glorifications:
Why Leaders are Depleted

Listen, most women leaders I know have challenging habits. Most leaders I know have come to justify and glorify five things. These five glorifications undermine our ability to stand fully in our purpose as leaders. They undermine our ability to grow our profits, destroy our relationships, and demolish our teams. I was a five-glorification master! Most leaders I know learn the glorifications through our leadership role models.

As leaders, we learn how to lead from other leaders. Unfortunately, the role models many of us look to are five-glorification masters. The five things we glorify are sacrifice, excessive hours, illness, "on" 24-hours, and exhaustion.

Now, I've struggled as I've thought about these glorifications. There are conversations about leadership that say something like, "You're not going to be successful unless you're working 80, 90 or 100 plus hours a week. You won't be successful if you take time off to take care of your physical health because you're going to lose traction. You're going to lose market share. You're won't be successful if you don't make sacrifices. You'll never get promoted if you leave to see your children. You can't be successful if you're not "on" and accessible 24/7 especially in our global marketplace.

We're encouraged to sacrifice sleep and rest all in the name of being accessible to clients around the world.

Imagine how these five glorifications undermine your purpose as a leader, minimize your profits, and negatively impact your team and other important relationships.

Sacrifice

When I first started building a multi-million dollar organization, I remember sitting down and having a conversation with myself that went something like this: "Jenny, you're an extraordinary and creative woman. You are deeply connected to your spiritual practice, you love to be outside, and you love new ideas and new ways to be creative, and new ways to move people.

But Jenny, this organization you're building is going to require sacrifice—lots of sacrifice. You're going to have to stay really focused, laser focused and very disciplined. You're going to need to sacrifice your creativity because if you spend too much time in your creativity

From Empty to Overflow

Jenny, you're going to be all over the place. And people need stability, direction, certainty.

When did I learn that? Well, I served in the military as a United States Marine.

As a Marine, sacrifice is one way we're encouraged to lead by example. We take care of our people first then we get to ourselves. Now, I understand the rationale in the military context because it is very important for senior leaders to make sure that their people are cared for well.

Why? Because our people are mission critical. Your job as leader is to make sure that your people are fed, that they're as comfortable as possible, they get their mail if you're in the field. So, that made sense. But that model is a model for a specific context. This idea of sacrifice was one that I took and repurposed to a different context. I didn't understand that sacrifice must be looked at very carefully.

I absolutely believe in leading by example. However, what I learned was that I used "sacrifice" as a way of avoiding being fully present in my life, as well as, engaging and trusting my team.

Excessive

How many times have you said or heard leaders say, "Oh man, I'm putting in an all-nighter tonight! I gotta get this project done and I'm on my third day of all-nighters!"

Our eyes get big because we can't imagine the superhuman effort that it takes to do that. Then we question ourselves: Will I be successful if I don't put in more hours? Then we might try to mirror the same broken behavior.

From Empty to Overflow

I routinely worked 16 – 18 hour days. Yes, that would often include weekends. My schedule: stay at work until 7:00 or 8:00pm. Then head home. I might eat and then I'd do a little more work until I just literally passed out. Many mornings, I would wake up at 1:00am—heart-pounding. As I bolted awake, I'd be in a panic thinking of all the things that I didn't do or that I needed to do. I hurled from crisis to crisis.

Sometimes my mind was racing so fast, I couldn't sleep. I'd start working at 2 o'clock in the morning, then by 6:00am, I'd jump into my car and drive to work.

These early morning work sessions had me sending emails to everyone—my staff, board, colleagues. Originally, I did this just to get stuff off my plate so I wouldn't have to continue thinking about whatever it was. But by doing it, I created the idea with my team that we all needed to act like superheroes.

Jenny DuFresne

Through my actions, I conveyed to them the message that we needed to be on 24/7 and that there was nothing in our lives but work. I saw this affect the people that stayed around and I also saw it drive people away.

The glorification of excessive hours lead me to drive myself into the ground. I was perpetually depleted, exhausted. Our bodies are an amazing system. But our body is not a robot. To sustain optimal functioning, we need healthy eating, rest, and exercise, spiritual and relational connection. All are non-negotiable. As I glorified excessive hours, my body began to breakdown. Small breakdowns at first. It was here I began to glorify physical illness.

Illness
How many of you right now have not been to the doctor for a year or more?

From Empty to Overflow

Several years ago, I would raise my hand. Proudly. My weird, warped badge of honor. Listen, when I was in the middle of building a multi-million dollar organization, I repeatedly said that I didn't have time to go to the doctor. I didn't have time for my annual checkups. I didn't have time to take care of bodily ailments. I didn't want to spend the time dialing my doctor's number to make an appointment. I just didn't have time. It was six years later, when I finally did make time. By that time, I had done tremendous damage to my body.

This is one way we glory physical illness and our inflated sense of invulnerability. I don't have time to take care of myself by going to the doctor. The reality was, I didn't want to hear what the doctor had to say.

Most of us don't act because we're scared to death that the doctor's going to tell us that we're overdoing, overworking, and over stressing our body. We're afraid the doctor will tell us our bodies are not handling our abuse well. Or, the doctor will tell us we've been consuming foods that are not healthy for us and so our body is revolting by onset diabetes, heart-problems, or other quality-of-life altering ailments.

The other way we glorify physical illness (and our "commitment" to success) is we come to work sick. Again, I'm guilty—very guilty.

For several years, I would get respiratory bacterial and viral infections. I would keep pushing, no rest, and no change in my stress level.

One year, I developed acute chronic bronchitis. It wasn't the first time. It might have been the 15th time. It got progressively worse. I would run to Urgent Care because that's the place where "busy" people go. The doctor would say, "You have chronic bronchitis." They would give me antibiotics. I was in the throes of the highest stress I had experienced building the organization.

The first round of antibiotics didn't cure the bronchitis. Over the course of the next six-months, I was on three rounds of antibiotics increasingly more potent and more powerful, but I didn't get well. Then came the breathing machines as my breathing became more compromised.

I would drag myself into work. Here again, I'm the role model for people around me. I would drag myself into work weak, trembling, practically green and barely able to breathe.

I would muster some thread of energy. And put it all on the line. I would work even harder. I would prove I wasn't weak. I was tough. My staff would just look at me. I reveled in the look of awe—not seeing the look of pity. I refused to hear their admonishments to go home. "So much to do!" I'd chant. I can't afford to be sick.

But because I was in the glorification of physical illness, I was like, "Yeah, I can push through this. It's not a problem." I didn't take care of myself, and I was a terrible example to the people around me. That chronic bronchitis, that six months of it was the longest period. I would generally have bronchitis and things associated with it like horrible flu. But, I would keep pushing oblivious to the damage I was doing.

Do you see yourself here? Your body is telling you through sickness that it needs a break. It needs rest. It needs a day or week off. Your body tells you when it is depleted and that it doesn't have the energy necessary. It needs a break. But we like to glorify being accessible.

Accessible

As leaders, we have learned that if we're not accessible, meaning someone can't see us, call us, email us and we don't respond within 10 minutes, that somehow, we're not good enough; that we are slacking as leaders.

I think this happens particularly with women in leadership roles.

We have glorified being accessible. "Call me, I'm available 24 hours." "My phone is right beside my bed, it's on. If you need me just text me." Right? What impact does it have on your family? What impact does that have on your team? I found that my team became less able to solve problems on their own. They're fully capable of solving problems on their own, but because they knew I was accessible, they second guessed themselves.

24-hour accessibility is ridiculous. Imagine how demoralizing it is to your team to always feel like they're not doing enough; that they must choose between enjoying life, contributing at a high level, or looking for another job. The glorification of accessibility undermines our team from adding tremendous value to the important people in their lives and *still* making the mission happen. The glorification of being accessible keeps us in the glorification of exhaustion.

Exhaustion
Again, this goes back to working hours and hours, existing on two or three hours of sleep, and waking up in the middle of the night because a text message or an email came through.

From Empty to Overflow

We have our devices beside our bed, and they're on. So, we always hear these pings, dings, and alerts from people across the country, around the world, or other people who are stressed out because we've been role modeling for them the way they should be as employees or as leaders.

I can't tell you the number of people that used to look at me or would say to me after one of my 2:00am email sessions, "Oh my gosh, I can't believe you sent an email at two in the morning! I looked at the time stamp on that." But they would look at me with some mixed of awe and fear and something like, "Wow, I don't know if I can keep up with her. She's a beast. She's a machine." Have you seen that? Has your ego ever been stroked by a comment or that look of awe? Unfortunately, mine was.

The glorification of exhaustion is something I see entrepreneurs and leaders do with abandon. We glorify being exhausted and existing on very little sleep. We glorify the "grind". But the challenge is that all those things lead us to being completely empty. When we're walking around as empty vessels, we make terrible decisions. We make sleep-deprived, frustrated, exhausted decisions. Those decisions impact everything—our close relationships, our team, our profits.

When we glorify exhaustion, we're trying to show people that we've got it together; that we're strong and robust. We're invincible. All of this is just a fabrication. I'm committed to shining a spotlight on this idea that we must lead empty to be successful. I am crystal clear that when we do better, when we lead from our overflow, the world is better.

From Empty to Overflow

Chapter 4:

From Empty to Overflow

My commitment is to share the ways we can reinvent our lives, put radical self-care at the center, so we can ignite our purpose; maximize our profits; and inspire the people around us. We don't win any awards. We don't receive great accolades by glorifying sacrifice, excessive hours, being 100% accessible, being sick, or exhausted. The five glorifications are a simple recipe for death—relational, spiritual, creative, profits, or physical.

My Stand

I invite you to join this journey as I share five radical actions I discovered. These radical self-care actions allow me to cultivate my energy to overflow and lead powerfully. My stand for you is that you lead from joy, happiness, purpose, passion. My stand is that this is the way you serve the world by sharing your amazing gifts as a leader. When we lead with our absolute best selves we role model rest, rejuvenation, reconnection, relationships, passion, and purpose.

Anything else is a myth. Success without joy, happiness, and vitality is empty. I have discovered and know this truth: we can rest, serve revitalized, have joy AND tremendous success. We can be in a fulfilling relationship with ourselves— and have a powerful business.

As leaders embrace this idea, we'll be able to fulfill our missions and vision in powerful ways. Internally, we'll have the actual energy we need—both mentally and physically—to create overflowing success.

You'll have within you the joy that allows people to be close to you and want to be around you. Which in turn, positively impacts your profits. It impacts those people that you love. It inspires the team responsible for moving your company's mission forward. Of course, it also impacts the customers and clients you   serve.

Redefine Work

A false notion many of us bought into is that the harder we work, the more value we have. The more hours we spend, the more successful our business will be.

What has happened in our companies is that we (leaders) become the bottleneck to success. We feel we must do, see, and know everything. We are stressed out. We are not creative, fully present, or able to do the things that we could do because we're trying to do everything. Our exhausted, low-energy selves believe that we're sharp decision-makers on top of it all. But think for a minute. What kind of an impact will you make as a leader if you're fully energized, creative, in balance and harmony with yourselves and with others?

As women in leadership roles, we often tell ourselves that we're lazy when we're not working. But really, we need to have time when we're off. It doesn't make us lazy to take care of ourselves or to rest. We no longer need to sacrifice joy, people and relationships that are important to us. We no longer need to sacrifice our health just to get one more thing done—to answer just one more email.

Chapter 5:

5 Radical Actions to Go from Empty to Overflow

You might be asking yourself, "So how do I do this? How do I lead from my overflow?" I hope by now that this is something you want to do. But now we need to talk practically. How can you go from running on empty to leading from your overflow?

I discovered and use five actions daily. These radical actions enable me and the leaders I coach to lead from an abundant overflow. Below are the actions in brief. For more information and resources, please visit the site:
www.FromEmptytoOverflow.com.

I find it helpful to share a question for each life-changing, radical action. The question is the beginning of your opportunity to structure your life to lead from your overflow. The five actions are **_rest, release, rejuvenate, refocus, and reconnect_**.

Rest

No, rest and sleep are **_not_** overrated. When we get a full seven or eight hours of sleep every night, we treat ourselves better and we make better decisions. By extension, we treat our families better, and they treat other people better. By extension of that, when we go to work we treat our employees better, and that maximizes our profits because there's a freedom that's flows through us and our team. We are absolutely at our best when we are well-rested.

My shero, Arianna Huffington, the Founder of Huffington Post, is a staunch advocate of sleep. She sparked a new stand for people to get at least 7-hours of sleep. She writes...

"Of course it's not just technology that comes between us and a good night's sleep. It's also our collective delusion that overwork and burnout are the price we must pay in order to succeed. Feeling that there aren't enough hours in the day, we look for something to cut. And sleep is an easy target. In fact, up against this unforgiving definition of success, sleep doesn't stand a chance."

Question: What conditions do you need to create to sleep 7 to 8 hours each night?

Reconnect

Reconnect with what matters most: your important relationships. This action fills you with boundless energy. When was the last time you had a massage? Do you have a date night with your spouse or date day with your children? When was the last time you had coffee with your friends? When you're with the important relationships in your life go digital free. Silence your cellphone and close your laptop. Trust me...the world will not end!

Start each week intentionally scheduling time with each of your soul-filling relationships. Date night, date day, game night—really the opportunities to connect with people you love are endless. Or maybe it's time to connect and create a new love if you're single.

Question: What or who nurtures your Spirit?

Release

Release is a reflective experience. If you look at your life think about those activities, people, to-do lists, or experiences that are robbing you of energy. Here's one that might be a bear for you: cleaning house. I love a clean, organized space. It helps me think clearer and feel settled. When I was working over 100-hours a week, my house became messier and messier.

My internal chatter demanded that I clean the house. Other activities were more demanding. I was resistant to hiring a house-keeper. But in the end, I did. Why? I had to release myself from the energy consuming mental chatter. The reality was I didn't want to spend my time cleaning my house. When I released myself and hired an amazing housekeeper, I literally felt free. I felt like I was given an endless supply of new energy.

From Empty to Overflow

When things are not going well, instead of continuing to ram your way out of the problem, stop. Take a minute. Breath. Realize that you are not a failure. Know that you are still worthy and it is okay for things not to not be completely clear. By doing this, we allow our genius (or the genius of others) to create totally new solutions.

Question: What can I release that no longer serves me?

Rejuvenate

Have fun! Create joy! The more intense our leadership roles, the more important fun, joy, laughter are to sustain and replenish our energy. It is so easy to sacrifice fun, joy, and happiness by being "too busy". Fun is a great abundant energy-creator. There is no time in your life where you should sacrifice fun and enjoyment in the pursuit of success.

Jenny DuFresne

A friend recently shared a story about her millionaire friend. This friend built an amazing company selling natural cosmetics. Before she launched her company, she went camping each weekend with friends from college; enjoyed yoga classes several times a week; and volunteered at a local animal shelter. All activities that created joy and fun in her life.

Her bank account was stuffed with cash, but now she felt miserable. Her friendships had drifted away, as well as the laughter, comfort, and memories. She rarely got to the yoga studio and her body was always taut with stress and anxiety. It had been months since a shelter dog barked in excitement to see her.

She was an exhausted, flat, uninteresting millionaire.

Fun is a non-negotiable necessity in your busy life.

Question: What is the highest joy producing activity that I can do this week?

Refocus

Working excessive hours, which I define as beyond 8-hours, drains your energy.

Design your day with frequent breaks to refocus your brain. Step away from your desk. Take a walk. Get outside into fresh air. When you refocus by allowing your brain to rest for 10 or 15-minutes, you create the opportunity to see problems with fresh eyes. We are in an illusion that suggests if we push harder we'll get farther. That is false. There's no honor in pushing yourself to a breaking point.

When you spend time thorough out the day connecting to your passions, you are helped to refocus on what is the most important thing. It also helps you focus on where your attention needs to be at the moment.

Question: What am I passionate about today?

No Excuses

Now that I've shared this list with you, I'm sure that you have a mountain of excuses for why you can't do it. My mantra was always, "I don't have enough time." "I'm too busy." "They won't respect me." "They will think I'm lazy or not committed."

That's all BS! Step off the treadmill for a moment. I challenge you to question why *any* of this is true. Are you lazy? Do you lack commitment? Even deeper— why does the opinion of other people matter to you?

In my experience, being driven by what I "thought" others thought about me was my personal recipe for disaster.

Our lives depend on our courageous, radical action to begin to create a different relationship with work and time. We can do something magical. We can create time.

Chapter 6:

Create Time

You may have an internal conversation about how much you need to be involved. The conversation may sound like this: "Listen, my team (or person) just isn't smart enough to know how to do this. I keep teaching them, but they just don't understand." This conversation happens more often than you realize. In your exhaustion, you may decide that your team isn't smart enough or they don't know what they're doing. To get the results you want, you must take over. This is FALSE. And it is your slippery slope to exhaustion, burnout, frustration—and absolutely no control over your time.

If we trust our people, allow them to try things and even to fail. If, as leaders, we loosen our fist and give our staff space, they can grow. This level of transparency also allows them to see that you're human and you have struggles. In that way, your team can engage and solve problems creatively. If you want your team to function like owners give them the opportunity to feel a sense of ownership. Your company and profits grow exponentially when your team feels effective and committed to achieving results.

As a leader, we sometimes don't see how our ineffective habits are driving down our profits or chasing our staff away. This may be where a leadership coach can support you to create productive habits and help you discover your blind spots.

At this moment, if you lack time for self-care—create it. You are the master your schedule, not the other way around. Think about it this way; if you don't take care of you or you burn yourself out, how much time will you have then? What is your quality of life after a heart attack or stroke? Time is your most precious asset.

How do you create time? Sit down with your calendar on a weekly basis. Schedule the 5 radical actions into your daily/weekly activities. Book time for *rest, release, rejuvenate, refocus,* and **reconnect**. If you find an internal battle with the "need" to prioritize work that is an opportunity to deeply look at why. Is there something that you're avoiding? Have you drifted away from your important relationships? Are you worried about the opinions of colleagues? Do you think your next promotion is in jeopardy? Unpack the reasons why and release them. Your greatest success is found in the 5 radical actions. Once you've scheduled the 5 radical actions, then fit everything else around them.

Be Present

One of the hardest things I had to recognize was that being fully present in my relationships and in my gifts, is what's important. You may have an amazing resume, like I do, but nobody really cares about a resume.

Working hard, putting all your energy into work can become the worst kind of loneliness. What I learned was that the overflow of energy I wanted to fuel everything came from being connected to the people around me. I believe living with joy is the deepest form of connection to life and people that we can aspire to create.

Today I work with leaders just like you (and me!). I help women leaders connect with themselves and reconnect the family, friends, and experiences that matter the most in life. Our relationships are crucial to leading from our overflow. I'm excited at this phase of my life where I can use my gifts to transform how we lead.

Today I lead by example. I lead from my overflow. I'm committed to creating space and opportunity for women leaders to envision and chart a new path. Now is the time for us to live fulfilling lives and leave stressed and empty lives behind.

I believe women leaders are the key to a thriving planet, productive communities, and enjoyable work environments.

Possibility and Power in the Overflow
As women leaders and entrepreneurs, we sometimes have a lone wolf attitude. We don't know how to look for or ask for help. Have you noticed that the goal or success we pursue keeps moving? Have you ever rested after reaching a goal? Or just celebrated, basked, shared, laughed after reaching a goal?

From Empty to Overflow

The leaders I work with are so driven that when the goal or success is approached, they move the goal or ignore it altogether. The truth should be the opposite. We push so hard that we will sacrifice anything—our health, relationships, and our teams—in the drive for the goal or success.

There are amazing possibilities living from our overflow. I believe we can create and embrace a different relationship with time that is radically different than anything we've lived.

Time is our most precious asset. We need a 360-degree relationship that starts with our **self-care first**. We need to take care of our bodies. We need rest—natural rest—without the help of drugs, alcohol, or other substances. We need to cultivate our inner life and light through creative endeavors. We need to take care of our families and friends because they energize us. Not just do things for them, but be fully present in our relationship with them. Experience, create, and share love. The beauty of our lives is interconnected to sustaining the relationships that nurture us.

Success **first** begins with radical self-care. My new definition of success embraces being happy, whole, and connected to what truly matters—our health, our families, our friends, our important relationships. That's what I'm committed to manifesting in the world by partnering with leaders to guide this redefinition of success.

My vision is that women leaders profoundly impact our planet. There is turmoil, uncertainty, and ambiguity in the world today. So much competes for our attention. I believe that women leaders are the transformers and global change-makers humanity needs—now.

Yes, we can create extraordinary profits, build great companies, and employ and inspire people. We do this and more when we lead from our overflow. To lead from our overflow, we must consciously replace the five dysfunctions I explored—*sacrifice, excessive hours, illness, accessible,* and *exhaustion*—with the five radical actions—*rest, reconnect, release, rejuvenate, refocus.*

This quote by Mahatma Gandhi inspires the five radical actions that I hope you—a woman leader—will embrace. The world needs us now more than ever.

> **"We but mirror the world. All the tendencies present in the outer world are to be found in the world of our body. If we could change ourselves, the tendencies in the world would also change. As a man [woman] changes his [her] own nature, so does the attitude of the world change toward him [her]. This is the**

divine mystery supreme. A wonderful thing it is and the source of our happiness. We need not wait to see what others do."

Thank you for your willingness to be a different kind of leader. Thank you for investing in creating your overflow. Thank you for being the leader who takes a step back and allows your staff to step forward—to learn and grow.

Please visit:
www.FromEmptytoOverflow.com
for receive tips and insights so you can lead powerfully from your overflow.

Made in the USA
Middletown, DE
23 September 2025